1,000 Words to
Ignite Romance

FLASH FICTION LIVE PRESENTS
101 ROMANCE WRITING
PROMPTS & CHALLENGES

1,000 Words to Ignite Romance

FLASH FICTION LIVE PRESENTS
101 ROMANCE WRITING
PROMPTS & CHALLENGES

CHANDRA ARTHUR & NATALIE LOCKE

INIMITABLE
BOOKS
UNFORGETTABLE STORIES

Published by Inimitable Books, LLC
www.inimitablebooksllc.com

1,000 WORDS TO IGNITE ROMANCE.
Copyright © 2025 by Chandra Arthur & Natalie Locke.
All rights reserved. Printed in China.

Library of Congress Cataloguing-in-Publication Data is available.

First edition, 2025
Cover design by Mandi Lynn of River Bend Books

ISBN 978-1-958607-23-7 (paperback)
10 9 8 7 6 7 6 5 4 3 2 1

To my chosen sister, Chandra, without whom I wouldn't want to take this trip.

~

To Natalie, for always saving me from my literary self.

1,000 Words to *Ignite Romance*

How to Use This Book:

Artistic license has never been more steamy than with an all-new installment in the *1,000 Words* series with 101 prompts and challenges that can go in any direction. You can fill in the prompts' blanks with as many words as you want. There are plenty of pages, so you can write in the book or type elsewhere.

Free yourself of expectations when working on these creative writing prompts. Don't be afraid to try new things with voice and your characters. Unlike the first book in the *1,000 Words* series, the provided words and prompts are targeted to help you write a romance flash fiction. If you like, you can outline your story before you begin, or you can fly by the seat of your desk chair. With the 101 prompts, you have room to practice and perfect your voice.

Each book comes with 1,000 word stickers in the back, but you can always write your own. Use the words as your prompts or as the 10 words to put in the allotted space below each prompt. These are the 10 words to incorporate into your story. You can also use word packs with additional stickers, available through our publisher's online store, to broaden your vocabulary.

To be considered a "flash fiction," each written piece must not exceed 1,000 words.

If you're looking for more structure, you can combine a prompt with one of the challenges by writing a challenge number in the box next to each prompt.

You can skip around in completing the prompts and challenges as you see fit. You do not need to complete them in chronological order as they are printed in the book.

Even though the romance requires a happy ever after (HEA), you do not need to adhere to this genre expectation in your flashes because there is always angst at some point in a romance story.

Tip to make prompts conflict based:
• Negate a verb: e.g. "can" becomes "cannot" / "can't"
"I can't love my friend" carries differently than "I can love my friend" or "Shouldn't love my friend"

Tips to make prompts character based:
• Abilities (lack of, or expert level—affects who your character will be around and how they will be treated)
• Focused on the past or a daydreamer of the future?
• Profession (how does it affect relationships?)
• Relationships (how do others feel about the romance?)
• Goals (working towards, achieved, fail but gain something else?)
• Age/maturity level (will it change at the end?)

1,000 Words to *Ignite Romance*

- Blend into a crowd or stand out? (looks-wise)
- What distinguishable personality traits do they have? (Opinionated, extrovert, quiet, workaholic, different project each week, etc)
- What is their flaw in a relationship? (closed off, untrusting, clingy, a runaway, etc.)
- What do they bring to the relationship table that the other person needs? (security, acceptance, stability, fun, fresh start)

i.e. A real estate agent meets new people every day and is always ready to network. They meet a full-time surfer who is a go-with-the-flow person. The surfer helps the real estate agent take a step away from work and relax while the agent helps the surfer set roots somewhere and finally stops running from commitment. The real estate agent recognizes although tomorrow isn't promised, it doesn't mean every relationship milestone must be hit today.

In some instances, it might be best to pick the challenge before the words.

Writing Challenges:

1. At the end of the love story, reveal that it all happened in the main character's head after first laying eyes on their love
2. Write a story from both love interests' POVs and end just before their meet cute
3. Write a historical romance
4. Gender-bend a famous couple (real or fictional)
5. Write a flash where the characters interact without talking
6. Write about sparking a new love in old age
7. Write about puppy love
8. Write about the worst first date with the best person
9. Write a meet cute in an unlikely place
10. Write a sports-themed rivals-to-lovers flash
11. Write a declaration of love
12. Jump around a love story's timeline and write 2 different scenes between the same characters
13. Write a flash where the characters talk (handwritten or digitally) before meeting in person for the first time
14. Write the end of a love story
15. Write the moment the characters turn from "just friends" to something more in a "friends-to-lovers" story
16. Write from a third wheel or matchmaker's perspective
17. Write an event from both love interests' perspectives

1,000 Words to *Ignite Romance*

18. Write someone buying a gift for their significant other (but we never meet them on page)
19. Make one of the chosen 10 (sticker) words pause an argument between a couple
20. Write the characters accomplishing a task together while talking about something unrelated
21. Write an internet relationship
22. Write a blind date
23. Write a double date that ends up with the couples switching partners
24. Write an anniversary
25. Write a strange, but special, tradition
26. Write about how a character makes a bad day better
27. Write a couple where one saves the other
28. Write one character proposing to another
29. Write a character getting bad news
30. Write a character sharing a deep, dark secret
31. Write a character finding out about a lie
32. Write a character getting happy news
33. Write a surprise
34. Write a holiday romance
35. Write a character meeting their significant other's family for the first time
36. Write about someone confusing twins
37. Write two characters dancing together
38. Write a couple's meeting on one of the people's worst day
39. Write characters deciding where to eat

40. Have one of the characters forget something
41. Have a character's (or both characters') competitive side(s) come out
42. Have a character learn something about the love interest
43. Rekindle a previously lost romance
44. Include a hospital emergency
45. Write a summer love
46. Write a long-distance relationship
47. Write about a language barrier
48. Write about betrayal, but where love still burns
49. Write the characters remodeling a house or apartment
50. Have one of the characters achieve their dream
51. Have a character support another after failing something
52. Write an amicable end to a relationship
53. Write a story where love interests walk in each other's shoes (metaphorically)
54. Write about a first date as if it's a job interview
55. Write a first impression that proves to be correct
56. Write about love after death (can be about love after a death or a love story in the afterlife)
57. Have your characters doing a trust exercise
58. Create a world where everyone has a soulmate
59. Write in multiple points of view, and each switch reveals new details that the other POVs didn't
60. Use the phrase "us against the world"
61. Write a throuple (a romantic or sexual relationship between 3 people)

1,000 Words to *Ignite Romance*

62. Write about love interests tackling each other's demons

63. Write a story where adults act like children

64. Have your couple choose the name for something (child, pet, car. etc.)

65. Write an international relationship

66. Write the only-one-bed trope, but it's not a mattress

67. Have your characters remember something differently, but both swearing *they* are correct

68. Take a side character from a different flash fiction you've written so far and write *their* love story

69. Write a story about self-love (not necessarily a euphemism, though it could be)

70. Write a physically intimate scene between characters

71. Write in 3rd person limited point of view

72. Write in 3rd person omniscient point of view

73. Describe characters eating (color, taste, texture, etc.)

74. Have your characters say the exact same words as each other, but with different emotional meanings

75. Write a story where one of the characters is sleeping

76. Have your story's timeline last only 1 minute

77. Use as many romance clichés as possible in your story

78. Avoid using the words *like, love, soulmate, fall, romance, affection, passion, lust,* and *yearn* as the characters fall for each other

79. Write 2 paranormal characters pretending to be human as they fall in love

80. Rewrite a horror story as a romance

81. Write a story where love isn't enough
82. Write a Happily Ever After for a couple
83. Write the epilogue to a love story
84. Write a dual universe where a split decision could bring the characters together or make them never meet at all
85. Have one character watch another struggle
86. Write about two villains falling in love
87. Write about an arranged marriage
88. Write about a doomed love
89. Write about a love story at the end of the world
90. Write multiple love stories existing in the same world
91. Rewrite a love story (if it's originally a couple being happy together, make it a break-up, and vice versa)

Writing Environment Challenges:

92. Listen to a breakup song while writing a love story, or listen to a song about falling in love while writing a break-up for your characters
93. Act out a scene before you write it (you can play all characters, or enlist others to help)
94. Write while lying down
95. Write in a romantic setting
96. Write in a coffee shop and base your characters off the other customers you see
97. Read a love poem before your writing session
98. Remain stoic as you write an emotional scene

1,000 Words to *Ignite Romance*

99. Write your story in the bathroom (and congratulate yourself if you finish it before someone comes knocking)
100. Write outside (be sure to wear weather-appropriate clothes—we're not asking you to torture yourself)
101. Write while traveling or commuting (plane, train, boat, or car—not while you're driving)

Happy writing and, again, don't forget to share your work online with us by using `#1000wordsprompt`.

Expand your word options by using your leftover stickers from other *1,000 Words* writing books.

x

1,000 Words to *Ignite Romance*

☐ The _____ day

```
.........................................................................
.........................................................................
```

1,000 Words to *Ignite Romance*

_____

_____

_____

_____

_____

_____

_____

_____

_____

_____

_____

_____

_____

_____

_____

_____

_____

_____

_____

_____

_____

_____

_____

_____

_____

_____

_____

_____

_____

_____

1,000 Words to *Ignite Romance*

I'll never _____

1,000 Words to *Ignite Romance*

_____

_____

_____

_____

_____

_____

_____

_____

_____

_____

_____

_____

_____

_____

_____

_____

_____

_____

_____

_____

_____

_____

_____

_____

_____

_____

_____

_____

_____

_____

_____

_____

1,000 Words to *Ignite Romance*

Advice for _____

1,000 Words to *Ignite Romance*

_____
_____
_____
_____
_____
_____
_____
_____
_____
_____
_____
_____
_____
_____
_____
_____
_____
_____
_____
_____
_____
_____
_____
_____
_____
_____
_____
_____

1,000 Words to *Ignite Romance*

☐ The _____
things we _____

```
................................................................
................................................................
```

_____
_____
_____
_____
_____
_____
_____
_____
_____
_____
_____
_____
_____
_____
_____
_____
_____
_____
_____
_____

_____
_____
_____
_____
_____
_____
_____
_____
_____
_____
_____
_____
_____
_____
_____
_____
_____
_____
_____
_____
_____
_____
_____
_____
_____
_____
_____

1,000 Words to *Ignite Romance*

_____

_____

_____

_____

_____

_____

_____

_____

_____

_____

_____

_____

_____

_____

_____

_____

_____

_____

_____

_____

_____

_____

_____

_____

_____

_____

_____

_____

_____

_____

_____

_____

_____

CHANDRA ARTHUR & NATALIE LOCKE

1,000 Words to *Ignite Romance*

Until _____

1,000 Words to *Ignite Romance*

_____
_____
_____
_____
_____
_____
_____
_____
_____
_____
_____
_____
_____
_____
_____
_____
_____
_____
_____
_____
_____
_____
_____
_____
_____
_____
_____
_____

1,000 Words to *Ignite Romance*

It was always _____

1,000 Words to *Ignite Romance*

1,000 Words to *Ignite Romance*

Sometimes _____
when _____

1,000 Words to *Ignite Romance*

_____
_____
_____
_____
_____
_____
_____
_____
_____
_____
_____
_____
_____
_____
_____
_____
_____
_____
_____
_____
_____
_____
_____
_____
_____
_____
_____
_____
_____

1,000 Words to *Ignite Romance*

The first time _____

_____
_____
_____
_____
_____
_____
_____
_____
_____
_____
_____
_____
_____
_____
_____
_____
_____
_____
_____
_____
_____
_____
_____
_____

1,000 Words to *Ignite Romance*

_____

_____

_____

_____

_____

_____

_____

_____

_____

_____

_____

_____

_____

_____

_____

_____

_____

_____

_____

_____

_____

_____

_____

_____

_____

_____

_____

_____

_____

_____

1,000 Words to *Ignite Romance*

I have to _____ goodbye

1,000 Words to *Ignite Romance*

_____

_____

_____

_____

_____

_____

_____

_____

_____

_____

_____

_____

_____

_____

_____

_____

_____

_____

_____

_____

_____

_____

_____

_____

_____

_____

_____

_____

_____

_____

1,000 Words to *Ignite Romance*

A _____ kiss

1,000 Words to *Ignite Romance*

_____
_____
_____
_____
_____
_____
_____
_____
_____
_____
_____
_____
_____
_____
_____
_____
_____
_____
_____
_____
_____
_____
_____
_____
_____
_____
_____
_____
_____
_____
_____

1,000 Words to *Ignite Romance*

We almost _____
find _____

....
....

_____
_____
_____
_____
_____
_____
_____
_____
_____
_____
_____
_____
_____
_____
_____
_____
_____
_____
_____
_____
_____

CHANDRA ARTHUR & NATALIE LOCKE

_____
_____
_____
_____
_____
_____
_____
_____
_____
_____
_____
_____
_____
_____
_____
_____
_____
_____
_____
_____
_____
_____
_____
_____
_____
_____

1,000 Words to *Ignite Romance*

_____

_____

_____

_____

_____

_____

_____

_____

_____

_____

_____

_____

_____

_____

_____

_____

_____

_____

_____

_____

_____

_____

_____

_____

_____

_____

_____

_____

_____

_____

1,000 Words to *Ignite Romance*

You _____

call a _____

:::

:::

1,000 Words to *Ignite Romance*

_____
_____
_____
_____
_____
_____
_____
_____
_____
_____
_____
_____
_____
_____
_____
_____
_____
_____
_____
_____
_____
_____
_____
_____
_____
_____
_____
_____
_____

1,000 Words to *Ignite Romance*

When I asked you _____,
you _____

....
....

1,000 Words to *Ignite Romance*

_____
_____
_____
_____
_____
_____
_____
_____
_____
_____
_____
_____
_____
_____
_____
_____
_____
_____
_____
_____
_____
_____
_____
_____
_____
_____
_____
_____

1,000 Words to *Ignite Romance*

☐ Our other _____ lives

1,000 Words to *Ignite Romance*

(ruled writing lines)

1,000 Words to *Ignite Romance*

My wish for _____
is that _____

_____
_____
_____
_____
_____
_____
_____
_____
_____
_____
_____
_____
_____
_____
_____
_____
_____
_____
_____
_____
_____
_____
_____
_____
_____

1,000 Words to *Ignite Romance*

_____

_____

_____

_____

_____

_____

_____

_____

_____

_____

_____

_____

_____

_____

_____

_____

_____

_____

_____

_____

_____

_____

_____

_____

_____

_____

_____

1,000 Words to *Ignite Romance*

☐ With all _____

1,000 Words to *Ignite Romance*

1,000 Words to *Ignite Romance*

☐ _____ when you
call, but _____

....
....

_____
_____
_____
_____
_____
_____
_____
_____
_____
_____
_____
_____
_____
_____
_____
_____
_____
_____
_____
_____
_____
_____

1,000 Words to *Ignite Romance*

_____

_____

_____

_____

_____

_____

_____

_____

_____

_____

_____

_____

_____

_____

_____

_____

_____

_____

_____

_____

_____

_____

_____

_____

_____

_____

_____

_____

_____

1,000 Words to *Ignite Romance*

☐ I'm sorry I _____

....
....

_____
_____
_____
_____
_____
_____
_____
_____
_____
_____
_____
_____
_____
_____
_____
_____
_____
_____
_____

1,000 Words to *Ignite Romance*

_____
_____
_____
_____
_____
_____
_____
_____
_____
_____
_____
_____
_____
_____
_____
_____
_____
_____
_____
_____
_____
_____
_____
_____
_____
_____
_____
_____
_____
_____

1,000 Words to *Ignite Romance*

If you could _____
when you see me _____

....
....

_____
_____
_____
_____
_____
_____
_____
_____
_____
_____
_____
_____
_____
_____
_____
_____
_____
_____
_____

1,000 Words to *Ignite Romance*

_____
_____
_____
_____
_____
_____
_____
_____
_____
_____
_____
_____
_____
_____
_____
_____
_____
_____
_____
_____
_____
_____
_____
_____
_____
_____
_____
_____
_____
_____
_____
_____

1,000 Words to *Ignite Romance*

They never _____ before

1,000 Words to *Ignite Romance*

1,000 Words to *Ignite Romance*

☐ We can't _____
  or _____

_____

....
....

_____
_____
_____
_____
_____
_____
_____
_____
_____
_____
_____
_____
_____
_____
_____
_____
_____
_____
_____

1,000 Words to *Ignite Romance*

1,000 Words to *Ignite Romance*

You _____

I always _____

....
....

_____
_____
_____
_____
_____
_____
_____
_____
_____
_____
_____
_____
_____
_____
_____
_____
_____
_____
_____
_____

_____
_____
_____
_____
_____
_____
_____
_____
_____
_____
_____
_____
_____
_____
_____
_____
_____
_____
_____
_____
_____
_____
_____
_____
_____

1,000 Words to *Ignite Romance*

1,000 Words to *Ignite Romance*

☐ _____ without
a _____

> . . . .
> . . . .

1,000 Words to *Ignite Romance*

_____

_____

_____

_____

_____

_____

_____

_____

_____

_____

_____

_____

_____

_____

_____

_____

_____

_____

_____

_____

_____

_____

_____

_____

_____

_____

_____

_____

_____

_____

_____

_____

_____

_____

_____

_____

_____

_____

1,000 Words to *Ignite Romance*

When we _____ together

1,000 Words to *Ignite Romance*

_____
_____
_____
_____
_____
_____
_____
_____
_____
_____
_____
_____
_____
_____
_____
_____
_____
_____
_____
_____
_____
_____
_____
_____
_____
_____
_____

1,000 Words to *Ignite Romance*

☐ I sing ——————————————
  our ——————————————

1,000 Words to *Ignite Romance*

1,000 Words to *Ignite Romance*

☐ I always _____
the way _____

1,000 Words to *Ignite Romance*

1,000 Words to *Ignite Romance*

☐ For _____,
  I'd _____

> ....
> ....

1,000 Words to *Ignite Romance*

_____
_____
_____
_____
_____
_____
_____
_____
_____
_____
_____
_____
_____
_____
_____
_____
_____
_____
_____
_____
_____
_____
_____
_____
_____
_____
_____
_____
_____

1,000 Words to *Ignite Romance*

If you could _____,
we _____

....
....

_____
_____
_____
_____
_____
_____
_____
_____
_____
_____
_____
_____
_____
_____
_____
_____
_____
_____
_____

1,000 Words to *Ignite Romance*

(ruled writing lines)

1,000 Words to *Ignite Romance*

☐ My only _____

....
....

_____
_____
_____
_____
_____
_____
_____
_____
_____
_____
_____
_____
_____
_____
_____
_____
_____
_____

1,000 Words to *Ignite Romance*

1,000 Words to *Ignite Romance*

☐ Kisses _____
after _____

1,000 Words to *Ignite Romance*

_____
_____
_____
_____
_____
_____
_____
_____
_____
_____
_____
_____
_____
_____
_____
_____
_____
_____
_____
_____
_____
_____
_____
_____
_____
_____
_____
_____

1,000 Words to *Ignite Romance*

☐ When I see _____

1,000 Words to *Ignite Romance*

1,000 Words to *Ignite Romance*

Our only _____
should _____

_____
_____
_____
_____
_____
_____
_____
_____
_____
_____
_____
_____
_____
_____
_____
_____
_____
_____
_____
_____
_____
_____
_____
_____
_____
_____
_____
_____

1,000 Words to *Ignite Romance*

_____

_____

_____

_____

_____

_____

_____

_____

_____

_____

_____

_____

_____

_____

_____

_____

_____

_____

_____

_____

_____

_____

_____

_____

_____

_____

_____

_____

_____

_____

_____

1,000 Words to *Ignite Romance*

☐ Climbing the _____

···
···

1,000 Words to *Ignite Romance*

_____
_____
_____
_____
_____
_____
_____
_____
_____
_____
_____
_____
_____
_____
_____
_____
_____
_____
_____
_____
_____
_____
_____
_____
_____
_____
_____
_____

1,000 Words to *Ignite Romance*

I should have _____,
but you _____

1,000 Words to *Ignite Romance*

_____
_____
_____
_____
_____
_____
_____
_____
_____
_____
_____
_____
_____
_____
_____
_____
_____
_____
_____
_____
_____
_____
_____
_____
_____
_____
_____

1,000 Words to *Ignite Romance*

Play for _____
my _____

1,000 Words to *Ignite Romance*

1,000 Words to *Ignite Romance*

Starting from _____

1,000 Words to *Ignite Romance*

_____
_____
_____
_____
_____
_____
_____
_____
_____
_____
_____
_____
_____
_____
_____
_____
_____
_____
_____
_____
_____
_____
_____
_____
_____
_____
_____

1,000 Words to *Ignite Romance*

My best _____
when I _____

....
....

_____
_____
_____
_____
_____
_____
_____
_____
_____
_____
_____
_____
_____
_____
_____
_____
_____
_____
_____
_____
_____
_____
_____

1,000 Words to *Ignite Romance*

1,000 Words to *Ignite Romance*

Music we _____
in the car _____

1,000 Words to *Ignite Romance*

_____
_____
_____
_____
_____
_____
_____
_____
_____
_____
_____
_____
_____
_____
_____
_____
_____
_____
_____
_____
_____
_____
_____
_____
_____
_____
_____
_____
_____

1,000 Words to *Ignite Romance*

☐ On _____ run
_____ with _____

....
....

_____
_____
_____
_____
_____
_____
_____
_____
_____
_____
_____
_____
_____
_____
_____
_____
_____
_____
_____
_____
_____

CHANDRA ARTHUR & NATALIE LOCKE

1,000 Words to *Ignite Romance*

_____
_____
_____
_____
_____
_____
_____
_____
_____
_____
_____
_____
_____
_____
_____
_____
_____
_____
_____
_____
_____
_____
_____
_____
_____
_____
_____
_____
_____

1,000 Words to *Ignite Romance*

The greenway _____

1,000 Words to *Ignite Romance*

1,000 Words to *Ignite Romance*

☐ Flying with _____

1,000 Words to *Ignite Romance*

_____

_____

_____

_____

_____

_____

_____

_____

_____

_____

_____

_____

_____

_____

_____

_____

_____

_____

_____

_____

_____

_____

_____

_____

_____

_____

_____

1,000 Words to *Ignite Romance*

Over the _____
and _____

_____

1,000 Words to *Ignite Romance*

1,000 Words to *Ignite Romance*

We _____
but _____

1,000 Words to *Ignite Romance*

_____

_____

_____

_____

_____

_____

_____

_____

_____

_____

_____

_____

_____

_____

_____

_____

_____

_____

_____

_____

_____

_____

_____

_____

_____

_____

_____

_____

1,000 Words to *Ignite Romance*

Orders come through _____
but _____

....
....

1,000 Words to *Ignite Romance*

_____
_____
_____
_____
_____
_____
_____
_____
_____
_____
_____
_____
_____
_____
_____
_____
_____
_____
_____
_____
_____
_____
_____
_____
_____
_____

1,000 Words to *Ignite Romance*

☐ _____ answer a
    call _____

```
..................................................
..................................................
```

_____
_____
_____
_____
_____
_____
_____
_____
_____
_____
_____
_____
_____
_____
_____
_____
_____
_____
_____
_____

1,000 Words to *Ignite Romance*

1,000 Words to *Ignite Romance*

☐ _____ in an email

1,000 Words to *Ignite Romance*

_____

_____

_____

_____

_____

_____

_____

_____

_____

_____

_____

_____

_____

_____

_____

_____

_____

_____

_____

_____

_____

_____

_____

_____

_____

_____

_____

_____

_____

1,000 Words to *Ignite Romance*

☐ A telegram from _____

1,000 Words to *Ignite Romance*

_____

_____

_____

_____

_____

_____

_____

_____

_____

_____

_____

_____

_____

_____

_____

_____

_____

_____

_____

_____

_____

_____

_____

_____

_____

_____

_____

_____

1,000 Words to *Ignite Romance*

☐ In the _____

family is _____

_____

_____

1,000 Words to *Ignite Romance*

_____
_____
_____
_____
_____
_____
_____
_____
_____
_____
_____
_____
_____
_____
_____
_____
_____
_____
_____
_____
_____
_____
_____
_____
_____
_____
_____
_____
_____
_____

1,000 Words to *Ignite Romance*

A dragon _____,
but tomorrow _____

_____
....
....

_____
_____
_____
_____
_____
_____
_____
_____
_____
_____
_____
_____
_____
_____
_____
_____
_____
_____
_____
_____

1,000 Words to *Ignite Romance*

_____
_____
_____
_____
_____
_____
_____
_____
_____
_____
_____
_____
_____
_____
_____
_____
_____
_____
_____
_____
_____
_____
_____
_____
_____
_____
_____
_____
_____
_____

1,000 Words to *Ignite Romance*

I don't _____

could update _____

_____

_____

_____

_____

_____

_____

_____

_____

_____

_____

_____

_____

_____

_____

_____

_____

_____

_____

_____

_____

CHANDRA ARTHUR & NATALIE LOCKE

1,000 Words to *Ignite Romance*

_____
_____
_____
_____
_____
_____
_____
_____
_____
_____
_____
_____
_____
_____
_____
_____
_____
_____
_____
_____
_____
_____
_____
_____
_____
_____
_____
_____
_____
_____
_____

1,000 Words to *Ignite Romance*

☐ _____ picture
on the _____

....
....

_____

_____

_____

_____

_____

_____

_____

_____

_____

_____

_____

_____

_____

_____

_____

_____

_____

_____

_____

1,000 Words to *Ignite Romance*

_____
_____
_____
_____
_____
_____
_____
_____
_____
_____
_____
_____
_____
_____
_____
_____
_____
_____
_____
_____
_____
_____
_____
_____
_____
_____
_____
_____
_____
_____
_____
_____

1,000 Words to *Ignite Romance*

☐ A reminder _____

_____
. . . .
. . . .
_____

_____
_____
_____
_____
_____
_____
_____
_____
_____
_____
_____
_____
_____
_____
_____
_____
_____
_____
_____

1,000 Words to *Ignite Romance*

_____

_____

_____

_____

_____

_____

_____

_____

_____

_____

_____

_____

_____

_____

_____

_____

_____

_____

_____

_____

_____

_____

_____

_____

_____

_____

_____

_____

_____

1,000 Words to *Ignite Romance*

☐ —————————————————— a warm
—————————————————— and tea

:..:
:..:

————————————————————————
————————————————————————
————————————————————————
————————————————————————
————————————————————————
————————————————————————
————————————————————————
————————————————————————
————————————————————————
————————————————————————
————————————————————————
————————————————————————
————————————————————————
————————————————————————
————————————————————————
————————————————————————
————————————————————————
————————————————————————

1,000 Words to *Ignite Romance*

_____
_____
_____
_____
_____
_____
_____
_____
_____
_____
_____
_____
_____
_____
_____
_____
_____
_____
_____
_____
_____
_____
_____
_____
_____
_____
_____
_____
_____
_____

1,000 Words to *Ignite Romance*

☐ Over a decade and _____

....
....

_____

_____

_____

_____

_____

_____

_____

_____

_____

_____

_____

_____

_____

_____

_____

_____

_____

_____

1,000 Words to *Ignite Romance*

1,000 Words to *Ignite Romance*

_____ long time
_____ before

_____

_____

_____

_____

_____

_____

_____

_____

_____

_____

_____

_____

_____

_____

_____

_____

_____

_____

_____

_____

_____

_____

_____

_____

1,000 Words to *Ignite Romance*

_____
_____
_____
_____
_____
_____
_____
_____
_____
_____
_____
_____
_____
_____
_____
_____
_____
_____
_____
_____
_____
_____
_____
_____
_____
_____

1,000 Words to *Ignite Romance*

You could _____,
and I would _____

_____
....
....

_____
_____
_____
_____
_____
_____
_____
_____
_____
_____
_____
_____
_____
_____
_____
_____
_____
_____

1,000 Words to *Ignite Romance*

_____
_____
_____
_____
_____
_____
_____
_____
_____
_____
_____
_____
_____
_____
_____
_____
_____
_____
_____
_____
_____
_____
_____
_____
_____
_____
_____
_____
_____
_____
_____

1,000 Words to *Ignite Romance*

☐ You never stay _____

_____

1,000 Words to *Ignite Romance*

_____
_____
_____
_____
_____
_____
_____
_____
_____
_____
_____
_____
_____
_____
_____
_____
_____
_____
_____
_____
_____
_____
_____
_____
_____
_____
_____
_____
_____
_____

1,000 Words to *Ignite Romance*

I believe _____,
but I could _____

1,000 Words to *Ignite Romance*

1,000 Words to *Ignite Romance*

☐ You, me, and _____

1,000 Words to *Ignite Romance*

1,000 Words to *Ignite Romance*

Wishing _____

is _____

_____

....

....

_____

_____

_____

_____

_____

_____

_____

_____

_____

_____

_____

_____

_____

_____

_____

_____

_____

_____

_____

_____

1,000 Words to *Ignite Romance*

_____

_____

_____

_____

_____

_____

_____

_____

_____

_____

_____

_____

_____

_____

_____

_____

_____

_____

_____

_____

_____

_____

_____

_____

_____

_____

_____

_____

CHANDRA ARTHUR & NATALIE LOCKE

1,000 Words to *Ignite Romance*

☐ Pour the _____
   I have _____

1,000 Words to *Ignite Romance*

_____

_____

_____

_____

_____

_____

_____

_____

_____

_____

_____

_____

_____

_____

_____

_____

_____

_____

_____

_____

_____

_____

_____

_____

_____

_____

_____

_____

_____

_____

_____

1,000 Words to *Ignite Romance*

[ ] _____ dinner,
but _____

. . . .	
. . . .	

_____
_____
_____
_____
_____
_____
_____
_____
_____
_____
_____
_____
_____
_____
_____
_____
_____
_____
_____

1,000 Words to *Ignite Romance*

_____

_____

_____

_____

_____

_____

_____

_____

_____

_____

_____

_____

_____

_____

_____

_____

_____

_____

_____

_____

_____

_____

_____

_____

_____

_____

_____

_____

_____

_____

_____

_____

1,000 Words to *Ignite Romance*

In the shop _____

1,000 Words to *Ignite Romance*

1,000 Words to *Ignite Romance*

☐ Pink _____
and purple _____

....
....

_____
_____
_____
_____
_____
_____
_____
_____
_____
_____
_____
_____
_____
_____
_____
_____
_____
_____
_____
_____

1,000 Words to *Ignite Romance*

_____
_____
_____
_____
_____
_____
_____
_____
_____
_____
_____
_____
_____
_____
_____
_____
_____
_____
_____
_____
_____
_____
_____
_____
_____
_____
_____
_____
_____
_____
_____

1,000 Words to *Ignite Romance*

☐ Blue _____
  feeling _____

: :
: :

_____

_____

_____

_____

_____

_____

_____

_____

_____

_____

_____

_____

_____

_____

_____

_____

_____

_____

_____

1,000 Words to *Ignite Romance*

_____
_____
_____
_____
_____
_____
_____
_____
_____
_____
_____
_____
_____
_____
_____
_____
_____
_____
_____
_____
_____
_____
_____
_____
_____
_____
_____

1,000 Words to *Ignite Romance*

☐ Just missed _____

_____

_____

1,000 Words to *Ignite Romance*

_____

_____

_____

_____

_____

_____

_____

_____

_____

_____

_____

_____

_____

_____

_____

_____

_____

_____

_____

_____

_____

_____

_____

_____

_____

_____

_____

_____

_____

_____

_____

1,000 Words to *Ignite Romance*

Poetically _____,
perfectly _____

1,000 Words to *Ignite Romance*

_____

_____

_____

_____

_____

_____

_____

_____

_____

_____

_____

_____

_____

_____

_____

_____

_____

_____

_____

_____

_____

_____

_____

_____

_____

_____

_____

_____

1,000 Words to *Ignite Romance*

Wish _____
and you _____

_____

. . . .
. . . .

_____
_____
_____
_____
_____
_____
_____
_____
_____
_____
_____
_____
_____
_____
_____
_____
_____
_____
_____
_____

1,000 Words to *Ignite Romance*

1,000 Words to *Ignite Romance*

☐ In my _____,
but not my _____

_____
....
....
_____

_____
_____
_____
_____
_____
_____
_____
_____
_____
_____
_____
_____
_____
_____
_____
_____
_____
_____

1,000 Words to *Ignite Romance*

_____

_____

_____

_____

_____

_____

_____

_____

_____

_____

_____

_____

_____

_____

_____

_____

_____

_____

_____

_____

_____

_____

_____

_____

_____

_____

_____

_____

_____

1,000 Words to *Ignite Romance*

That would have been _____

....
....

1,000 Words to *Ignite Romance*

1,000 Words to *Ignite Romance*

But _____

could go _____

1,000 Words to *Ignite Romance*

_____

_____

_____

_____

_____

_____

_____

_____

_____

_____

_____

_____

_____

_____

_____

_____

_____

_____

_____

_____

_____

_____

_____

_____

_____

_____

_____

_____

1,000 Words to *Ignite Romance*

☐ Don't apologize _____

_____
....
....
_____

_____
_____
_____
_____
_____
_____
_____
_____
_____
_____
_____
_____
_____
_____
_____
_____
_____
_____
_____
_____
_____
_____

1,000 Words to *Ignite Romance*

_____
_____
_____
_____
_____
_____
_____
_____
_____
_____
_____
_____
_____
_____
_____
_____
_____
_____
_____
_____
_____
_____
_____
_____
_____
_____
_____
_____
_____

1,000 Words to *Ignite Romance*

What I _____

was _____

1,000 Words to *Ignite Romance*

_____
_____
_____
_____
_____
_____
_____
_____
_____
_____
_____
_____
_____
_____
_____
_____
_____
_____
_____
_____
_____
_____
_____
_____
_____
_____
_____
_____
_____

1,000 Words to *Ignite Romance*

☐ _____ ,

yes _____

_____

_____

_____

_____

_____

_____

_____

_____

_____

_____

_____

_____

_____

_____

_____

_____

_____

_____

_____

1,000 Words to *Ignite Romance*

_____
_____
_____
_____
_____
_____
_____
_____
_____
_____
_____
_____
_____
_____
_____
_____
_____
_____
_____
_____
_____
_____
_____
_____
_____
_____
_____
_____
_____

1,000 Words to *Ignite Romance*

☐ Valentine's Day as a _____

....
....

1,000 Words to *Ignite Romance*

1,000 Words to *Ignite Romance*

A New Year's ———————————————
movie special

1,000 Words to *Ignite Romance*

_____
_____
_____
_____
_____
_____
_____
_____
_____
_____
_____
_____
_____
_____
_____
_____
_____
_____
_____
_____
_____
_____
_____
_____
_____
_____
_____
_____

1,000 Words to *Ignite Romance*

Lucky _____

and _____

1,000 Words to *Ignite Romance*

1,000 Words to *Ignite Romance*

☐ Thank you and _____

```
..............................................................................
..............................................................................
```

_____

_____

_____

_____

_____

_____

_____

_____

_____

_____

_____

_____

_____

_____

_____

_____

_____

_____

_____

_____

1,000 Words to *Ignite Romance*

1,000 Words to *Ignite Romance*

If _____ you _____
say _____

....
....

1,000 Words to *Ignite Romance*

1,000 Words to *Ignite Romance*

Special _____
for my _____

1,000 Words to *Ignite Romance*

1,000 Words to *Ignite Romance*

☐ I will _____
  after _____

```
...........................................................................
...........................................................................
```

_____
_____
_____
_____
_____
_____
_____
_____
_____
_____
_____
_____
_____
_____
_____
_____
_____
_____
_____

1,000 Words to *Ignite Romance*

_____
_____
_____
_____
_____
_____
_____
_____
_____
_____
_____
_____
_____
_____
_____
_____
_____
_____
_____
_____
_____
_____
_____
_____
_____
_____
_____
_____
_____

1,000 Words to *Ignite Romance*

☐ We _____
  in _____

1,000 Words to *Ignite Romance*

_____

_____

_____

_____

_____

_____

_____

_____

_____

_____

_____

_____

_____

_____

_____

_____

_____

_____

_____

_____

_____

_____

_____

_____

_____

_____

_____

_____

_____

_____

1,000 Words to *Ignite Romance*

☐ Watching _____
from _____

```
...........................................................................
...........................................................................
```

_____
_____
_____
_____
_____
_____
_____
_____
_____
_____
_____
_____
_____
_____
_____
_____
_____
_____
_____
_____

_____
_____
_____
_____
_____
_____
_____
_____
_____
_____
_____
_____
_____
_____
_____
_____
_____
_____
_____
_____
_____
_____
_____
_____
_____
_____

1,000 Words to *Ignite Romance*

_____

_____

_____

_____

_____

_____

_____

_____

_____

_____

_____

_____

_____

_____

_____

_____

_____

_____

_____

_____

_____

_____

_____

_____

_____

_____

_____

_____

1,000 Words to *Ignite Romance*

☐ Don't _____
go _____

_____

_____
_____

_____
_____
_____
_____
_____
_____
_____
_____
_____
_____
_____
_____
_____
_____
_____
_____
_____
_____
_____
_____

1,000 Words to *Ignite Romance*

_____
_____
_____
_____
_____
_____
_____
_____
_____
_____
_____
_____
_____
_____
_____
_____
_____
_____
_____
_____
_____
_____
_____
_____
_____
_____
_____
_____
_____
_____

1,000 Words to *Ignite Romance*

You are ———————————————————,
but so ———————————————————

1,000 Words to *Ignite Romance*

_____
_____
_____
_____
_____
_____
_____
_____
_____
_____
_____
_____
_____
_____
_____
_____
_____
_____
_____
_____
_____
_____
_____
_____
_____
_____
_____
_____
_____
_____
_____
_____

1,000 Words to *Ignite Romance*

Start _____,
and I _____,

::
::

1,000 Words to *Ignite Romance*

1,000 Words to *Ignite Romance*

☐ _____ cold and _____
but not _____

_____
....
....

_____
_____
_____
_____
_____
_____
_____
_____
_____
_____
_____
_____
_____
_____
_____
_____
_____
_____
_____
_____

1,000 Words to *Ignite Romance*

_____
_____
_____
_____
_____
_____
_____
_____
_____
_____
_____
_____
_____
_____
_____
_____
_____
_____
_____
_____
_____
_____
_____
_____
_____
_____
_____
_____
_____
_____
_____

1,000 Words to *Ignite Romance*

☐ Make a _____

> ....
> ....

_____
_____
_____
_____
_____
_____
_____
_____
_____
_____
_____
_____
_____
_____
_____
_____
_____
_____
_____

1,000 Words to *Ignite Romance*

1,000 Words to *Ignite Romance*

☐ Fill _____
   you _____

1,000 Words to *Ignite Romance*

_____
_____
_____
_____
_____
_____
_____
_____
_____
_____
_____
_____
_____
_____
_____
_____
_____
_____
_____
_____
_____
_____
_____
_____
_____
_____
_____
_____
_____
_____

1,000 Words to *Ignite Romance*

Footprints _____
by _____

1,000 Words to *Ignite Romance*

_____
_____
_____
_____
_____
_____
_____
_____
_____
_____
_____
_____
_____
_____
_____
_____
_____
_____
_____
_____
_____
_____
_____
_____
_____
_____
_____
_____

1,000 Words to *Ignite Romance*

In _____

hand _____

1,000 Words to *Ignite Romance*

_____
_____
_____
_____
_____
_____
_____
_____
_____
_____
_____
_____
_____
_____
_____
_____
_____
_____
_____
_____
_____
_____
_____
_____
_____
_____
_____
_____

1,000 Words to *Ignite Romance*

By the _____ and
_____ and _____

1,000 Words to *Ignite Romance*

1,000 Words to *Ignite Romance*

☐ The limelight ———————————— lovers

1,000 Words to *Ignite Romance*

_____
_____
_____
_____
_____
_____
_____
_____
_____
_____
_____
_____
_____
_____
_____
_____
_____
_____
_____
_____
_____
_____
_____
_____
_____
_____
_____
_____
_____

1,000 Words to *Ignite Romance*

For _____
and _____

_____
: :
: :
_____

_____
_____
_____
_____
_____
_____
_____
_____
_____
_____
_____
_____
_____
_____
_____
_____
_____
_____
_____
_____
_____

1,000 Words to *Ignite Romance*

1,000 Words to *Ignite Romance*

So you ——————————————————,
and I ——————————————————

1,000 Words to *Ignite Romance*

_____
_____
_____
_____
_____
_____
_____
_____
_____
_____
_____
_____
_____
_____
_____
_____
_____
_____
_____
_____
_____
_____
_____
_____
_____
_____
_____
_____

1,000 Words to *Ignite Romance*

☐ When you walk _____

....
....

_____

_____

_____

_____

_____

_____

_____

_____

_____

_____

_____

_____

_____

_____

_____

_____

_____

_____

_____

1,000 Words to *Ignite Romance*

1,000 Words to *Ignite Romance*

Meeting in the _____

for the _____

1,000 Words to *Ignite Romance*

1,000 Words to *Ignite Romance*

Don't be so _____,
we can _____

1,000 Words to *Ignite Romance*

_____
_____
_____
_____
_____
_____
_____
_____
_____
_____
_____
_____
_____
_____
_____
_____
_____
_____
_____
_____
_____
_____
_____
_____
_____
_____
_____
_____
_____
_____

1,000 Words to *Ignite Romance*

☐ _____ in your eyes

1,000 Words to *Ignite Romance*

1,000 Words to *Ignite Romance*

☐ One _____
  before _____

_____

⋯⋯⋯⋯⋯⋯⋯⋯⋯⋯⋯⋯⋯⋯⋯⋯⋯⋯⋯⋯⋯⋯
⋯⋯⋯⋯⋯⋯⋯⋯⋯⋯⋯⋯⋯⋯⋯⋯⋯⋯⋯⋯⋯⋯

_____
_____
_____
_____
_____
_____
_____
_____
_____
_____
_____
_____
_____
_____
_____
_____
_____
_____
_____
_____

1,000 Words to *Ignite Romance*

1,000 Words to *Ignite Romance*

☐ It _____
at the beginning

```
..................................................................................
..................................................................................
```

1,000 Words to *Ignite Romance*

_____

_____

_____

_____

_____

_____

_____

_____

_____

_____

_____

_____

_____

_____

_____

_____

_____

_____

_____

_____

_____

_____

_____

_____

_____

_____

_____

_____

1,000 Words to *Ignite Romance*

Writing Reflections:

_____
_____
_____
_____
_____
_____
_____
_____
_____
_____
_____
_____
_____
_____
_____
_____
_____
_____
_____
_____
_____
_____
_____
_____
_____
_____

Natalie's Acknowledgments:

I'd love to acknowledge our Flash Fiction Live attendees, who can laugh at us as much as we laugh at ourselves. A judge-free draft and edit zone wasn't what we set out to do. We just wanted to create different stories the fastest way possible, but it is because of you that it has evolved.

Thank you to Zara for taking a chance on us and letting our imaginations run wild with the possibilities of the *1,000 Words* series.

Thank you to Mandi Lynn for setting our series' book cover "uniform" with the first and modifying it for this version.

Chandra's Acknowledgments

To all our Flash Fiction Live attendees, friends, and family who have been so supportive. And to my partner.

Mandi Lynn, thank you for the beautiful cover art.

And Zara, by whose request I will keep this brief. I could say more, but this has to be under 1,000 words.

About the Authors

Chandra Arthur is a full-time rescue dog and cat mom. By day, she is an IT professional and a writer by night. She writes Science Fiction, Fantasy, and Historical fiction in full length novels, flash fiction, and everything in between. When Chandra isn't writing, you can find her pouring over a book, playing computer games, drinking coffee, and sometimes all three at once.

When Natalie isn't working, reading, or taking care of two kids and two dogs with her husband, she sacrifices even more of her sleep to write. Letting passion be her guide, she has drafted over two hundred and fifty flash fiction pieces in fourteen months. Now she hopes to invoke passion in others.

abandon	approve	beast	bounce
above	arch	beat	bound
absolve	argue	bed	box
absorb	arm	beg	brace
accompany	arrive	begin	brake
ace	ascend	believe	brave
act	ask	below	bread
action	assist	belt	break
administer	attach	bend	breath
adopt	attack	beside	bridge
adorn	attainable	better	brink
against	attempt	between	brow
age	aura	bind	brush
aim	avoid	bite	buck
air	back	blade	buckle
allergic	badger	blanket	build
allow	bag	blast	bundle
alone	balance	blind	burn
alpha	bald	blink	burrow
alter	band	bloom	bust
always	bane	blow	busy
ancient	bank	bluff	button
anew	banter	board	buzz
angry	basement	bold	cacophony
apart	bass	boom	call
apex	bat	bother	calm
Aphrodite	bath	bottom	cancel
apologize	battle	boulder	canopy

captivate	classic	converge	cup
capture	clean	coo	cupid
cardigan	clear	copy	curl
care	click	core	curve
caress	climb	cost	cut
carpet	cling	council	cycle
cascade	cloak	count	daily
caster	close	counter	danger
cat	closet	couple	dangle
catch	cloud	courage	dare
center	code	cover	darkness
century	coil	cower	dawn
chain	collapse	cozy	daydream
change	collar	crave	daze
chant	collide	crawl	dazzle
chaos	color	crazy	deal
charade	combine	crease	death
chase	come	crest	decal
check	comfort	crinkle	decide
cheek	concern	cripple	deep
chime	conclusion	crisis	defeat
chin	conflict	cross	demand
choke	connect	crumble	denial
chortle	conquer	cry	depth
chose	consider	cue	descend
chuckle	consume	cuff	desert
city	contain	cult	desire
clamp	control	cultivate	despise

dessert	eat	escape	fill
destroy	eavesdrop	escort	final
develop	echo	eternal	find
dial	ecstasy	everything	finish
diamond	efficient	excel	fire
dictate	either	excited	first
differ	elate	expand	flame
dig	electric	explain	flash
dirt	element	explode	flee
discover	elevator	explore	flight
discuss	eliminate	extort	flip
divulge	emboss	facade	float
done	embrace	face	flounder
double	emotion	fail	flow
douse	employ	faint	fluff
dove	engage	faith	flutter
down	enamor	fall	fly
drape	enchant	family	focus
dream	encompass	fawn	fog
drift	encourage	fear	fold
drink	encumber	feast	follow
drip	end	feather	fondle
drive	energy	feel	fool
drop	enjoy	feign	foot
drum	enlighten	feisty	forbidden
drunk	entice	field	force
dwell	entrap	fight	forever
eager	envelope	figure	forget

forgive	gasp	gripe	hinder
form	gaze	groan	hint
foster	gem	groove	hive
foul	ghost	ground	hold
found	giant	grow	hole
fragile	gift	growl	home
frame	ginger	guard	hone
freakout	glide	guide	hook
free	glimmer	guilt	hope
fresh	gloat	gulf	hover
fret	glutton	gullible	huddle
friend	gone	gust	huff
frost	goodbye	habitat	hug
fruit	gorge	hair	hum
frustrated	grab	hand	humble
fulfill	grace	hang	humiliate
fumble	grand	harass	hunt
fume	grasp	hard	hurl
fun	grateful	harmony	hustle
fungus	grave	haze	hydraulic
fuse	gravel	headline	ice
future	gravity	heal	idea
gaggle	graze	hear	ideal
game	greet	heart	idle
gander	grimace	height	illuminate
gap	grin	help	imagine
garden	grind	hem	impare
garner	grip	hilt	impartial

impudent	king	line	marinate
indecisive	kiss	linger	marvel
individual	knife	lip	master
inspire	knit	list	meal
instant	knock	listen	mean
instinct	know	litany	meander
integrate	knuckle	live	meaningful
internal	labyrinth	load	measure
intertwine	lacking	locate	meat
invade	last	lock	meet
invisible	latent	lone	melt
involve	laugh	long	memorize
jack	lavender	look	memory
jagged	lay	loose	mental
jail	layback	lord	mesh
jarring	layer	lose	miles
jest	lead	lost	mimic
job	learn	loud	mine
join	leather	love	minuscule
joke	leave	low	minute
jostle	left	lunar	mirror
journey	leg	lunch	moment
jump	leverage	mad	monk
keep	liar	magnetic	monster
key	license	manage	mood
kick	lift	manic	moon
kill	ligament	march	mooring
kind	lightning	marksmen	morph

mother	obscene	peace	position
motive	observe	peak	pour
move	obtuse	pearl	power
muffle	offer	peel	powerful
muscle	office	pendant	practice
muse	old	perform	present
muster	open	perry	press
mute	operate	pester	prevent
mystery	orbit	pew	prime
nail	order	piece	prison
name	other	pierce	project
nation	out	pillar	prompt
nature	outside	pilot	property
navigate	overt	pin	pull
neck	overwhelm	pipes	pullover
negotiate	own	planets	pulse
nervous	pack	plant	pummel
nest	pain	platonic	punish
never	pan	play	push
nibble	pander	please	quadruple
nice	pane	pleasure	quarters
nomad	panic	pluck	queen
normal	partly	pocket	quite
north	pass	point	race
nothing	passion	poke	rain
nudge	past	ponder	raise
nurture	path	pop	ramp
obligate	pause	port	ration

reach	retreat	ruin	sharp
read	return	rule	shatter
real	reverse	run	shave
reality	revive	runaway	shift
reap	revolting	sack	shimmer
reason	rid	safe	shine
rebuild	ride	same	shock
recall	right	sarcasm	shot
recline	righteous	satellite	should
red	ring	save	shout
reflect	rip	scam	shove
regret	ripe	scan	show
rehearse	ripple	scatter	shrink
rekindle	rival	scent	shutter
relax	river	scorn	sibling
release	road	scratch	side
relentless	roam	scream	sight
relive	robes	scrounge	sign
remember	rock	search	silence
remiss	rocket	secret	silhouette
remove	role	send	silk
renegade	roll	serve	similar
repay	room	sever	simulate
repeat	root	shadow	singe
request	rose	shake	sink
require	rough	shape	siren
rescue	row	shard	sit
resonate	royal	share	sizzle

ski	solid	stare	sudden
skill	sorrow	startle	suffer
skip	sough	starve	support
slap	soul	stash	survive
slate	sour	state	sway
sleep	sow	stay	sweat
sleeve	space	steal	sweater
slide	spare	steam	sweep
slip	spark	step	sweet
slither	spartan	stew	swell
sloth	spat	stick	sworn
slow	special	still	symphony
slurp	speed	stop	table
smack	spice	store	tail
small	spider	storm	take
smart	spill	stow	tale
smirk	spin	strain	tame
smoke	spiral	strand	taste
smooth	spirit	strengthen	team
smother	spoon	stretch	tear
snack	square	string	tease
snake	squeak	strive	temper
snap	squeeze	stroke	temple
snatch	squelch	struck	tendril
sneak	stache	struggle	tense
soar	stammer	stuck	tentative
soft	stand	stutter	test
solicit	star	suck	tether

thanks	tribulation	visit	wind
thief	triple	vital	whittle
throw	trouble	vulture	wing
ticket	trust	wacky	wink
tickle	tuck	waist	wipe
tide	tulip	wait	wisp
tie	tumble	waiver	with
tier	tunnel	wake	wither
tighten	twirl	war	wonder
tilt	twist	warm	work
timid	ugly	warn	world
tingle	understand	wash	wounded
tip	uneven	watch	wrap
tiptoe	unleash	way	wreck
together	unlock	weak	wrist
told	unravel	weary	yank
top	up	weave	yearn
topple	upheaval	web	yell
torrential	upset	weight	youth
toss	utmost	welcome	zeal
touch	use	west	zip
track	version	wheel	zone
traitor	vex	whimsy	
transfix	vibe	whip	
transform	victory	whisper	
trap	vigor	whole	
travel	viral	whimper	
trial	vision	win	